DRAMA CLASSICS

The Drama Classics series aims to offer the world's greatest plays in affordable paperback editions for students, actors and theatregoers. The hallmarks of the series are accessible introductions, uncluttered and uncut texts and an overall theatrical perspective.

Given that readers may be encountering a particular play for the first time, the introduction seeks to fill in the theatrical/ historical background and to outline the chief themes rather than concentrate on interpretational and textual analysis. Similarly the play-texts themselves are free of footnotes and other interpolations: instead there is an end-glossary of 'difficult' words and phrases.

The texts of the English-language plays in the series have been prepared taking full account of all existing scholarship. The foreign language plays have been newly translated into a modern English that is both actable and accurate: many of the translators regularly have their work staged professionally.

Under the editorship of Kenneth McLeish, the Drama Classics series is building into a first-class library of dramatic literature representing the best of world theatre.

Series editor: Kenneth McLeish

Associate editors:
Professor Trevor R. Griffiths, *School of Literary and Media Studies, University of North London*
Simon Trussler, *Reader in Drama, Goldsmiths' College, University of London*

DRAMA CLASSICS *the first hundred*

The Alchemist
All for Love
Amphitryon
Andromache
Antigone
Arden of Faversham
Bacchae
The Beaux Stratagem
The Beggar's Opera
Birds
Blood Wedding
Brand
The Broken Jug
The Changeling
The Cherry Orchard
Children of the Sun
El Cid
The Country Wife
Cyrano de Bergerac
The Dance of Death
The Devil is an Ass
Doctor Faustus
A Doll's House
Don Juan
The Duchess of Malfi
Edward II
Electra (Euripides)
Electra (Sophocles)
An Enemy of the
    People
Enrico IV
The Eunuch
Every Man in his
    Humour
Everyman
The Father
Faust
A Flea in her Ear
Frogs
Fuenteovejuna

The Game of Love
    and Chance
Ghosts
The Government
    Inspector
Hedda Gabler
The Hypochondriac
The Importance of
    Being Earnest
An Italian Straw Hat
The Jew of Malta
King Oedipus
The Learned Ladies
Life is a Dream
The Lower Depths
The Lucky Chance
Lulu
Lysistrata
The Magistrate
The Malcontent
The Man of Mode
The Marriage of Figaro
Mary Stuart
The Master Builder
Medea
Menaechmi
The Misanthrope
The Miser
Miss Julie
Molière
A Month in the
    Country
A New Way to Pay
    Old Debts
Oedipus at Kolonos
The Oresteia
Phaedra
Philoctetes
The Playboy of the
    Western World

The Revenger's
    Tragedy
The Rivals
The Robbers
La Ronde
The Rover
The School for
    Scandal
The Seagull
The Servant of Two
    Masters
She Stoops to
    Conquer
The Shoemaker's
    Holiday
Six Characters in
    Search of an
    Author
Spring's Awakening
Strife
Tartuffe
Thérèse Raquin
Three Sisters
'Tis Pity she's a
    Whore
Too Clever by Half
Ubu
Uncle Vanya
Volpone
The Way of the World
The White Devil
The Wild Duck
Women Beware
    Women
Women of Troy
Woyzeck
Yerma

*The publishers welcome
suggestions for further titles*

DRAMA CLASSICS

EVERYMAN

introduced by Simon Trussler

NICK HERN BOOKS
London

A Drama Classic

This edition of *Everyman* first published in Great Britain
as a paperback original in 1996 by Nick Hern Books Limited,
14 Larden Road, London W3 7ST

The text of *Everyman* is reprinted from the 'New Mermaids'
Three Late Medieval Morality Plays, edited by G.A. Lester,
by arrangement with A. & C. Black (Publishers) Ltd

Copyright in the introduction © 1996 by Nick Hern Books Limited

Typeset by Country Setting, Woodchurch, Kent TN26 3TB
Printed by Watkiss Studios Limited, Biggleswade SG18 9ST

A CIP catalogue record for this book is available from the
British Library

ISBN 1 85459 386 2

Introduction

Origins and Authorship of *Everyman*

Some scholars believe that *Everyman* is a translation of the Dutch play *Elckerlijc*, attributed to Petrus Dorlandus, a Carthusian monk. Others hold that the Dutch play is a translation from the English. A few even postulate a lost original from which both independently derived.

The present consensus is to give the Dutch version priority. Certainly the first edition in that language, printed in Delft around 1495, may have been as many as twenty years ahead of the first English printing. However, although the play is supposed to have reached the stage in England by the turn of the century, the first and second English editions survive only in fragmentary form. Our text is therefore based on the first of the two extant editions to have come down to us in a complete state, both from the press of John Skot, issued respectively between 1528-29 and 1530-35.

Everyman is among the earliest plays to have survived in a printed rather than manuscript form. In view of the Dutch connection, it is significant that the craft of printing, established in Germany by Gutenberg around 1450, had been flourishing in what is now Holland and Belgium well before William Caxton came to London from Bruges in 1476, to set up the first press in his native country. Printers in Antwerp were still exporting translations for the English market well beyond that date; and the scholarly editor A.C. Cawley believes that Laurence Andrewe, who worked as a translator for an Antwerp printer before setting up on his own account in London, is a possible candidate as author – or 'compiler', in the idiom of the time – of the English version of the play.

The first surviving play to be printed in English, around 1515, was Henry Medwall's *Fulgens and Lucrece*. This came from the press of John Rastell – himself a playwright, who was later to bring out editions of his own plays, of his son-in-law John Heywood's, and of John Skelton's *Magnificence*. All these were among the earliest English plays of acknowledged authorship, and this in itself distinguishes them as products of the emergent individualism of the time. Our uncertainty over the identity of the author or adaptor of *Everyman* suggests, conversely, its deeper roots in the past: for, with rare exceptions, medieval drama, like so much medieval art, remained anonymous – the expression (often the creation) of a collective rather than an individual sensibility.

Everyman: **What Happens in the Play**

God, looking out from Heaven over his creation, bemoans men's love of worldly riches and their unrighteous behaviour. Summoning his messenger Death, God instructs him to seek out Everyman, who must make ready for a pilgrimage, bearing his book of reckoning with him. Everyman, thinking of 'fleshly lusts and his treasure', has Death 'least in mind', and his accounts are all unclear. He begs and even tries to bribe Death for more time to make himself ready, but Death agrees only to let him try to find someone who will accompany him on the journey.

Despite initial protestations of loyalty, Fellowship, Kindred, and Cousin all refuse to go with Everyman, while Goods cannot even stir from where he lies, 'in corners, trussed and piled so high'. Although Good Deeds would be willing to make the journey, she is so weighed down by Everyman's sins that she cannot rise: if she is to regain her strength, Everyman must seek the help of her sister, Knowledge, in purging himself of his sins. Knowledge accordingly brings Everyman to the House of Salvation, where at the urging of Confession he scourges himself as a penitent. Good Deeds is now able to rise up, and Everyman, putting on the garment of contrition, finds that his book of reckoning is clear.

Good Deeds and Knowledge suggest that Everyman should ask Beauty, Strength, Discretion, and Five Wits to help him in his pilgrimage, as all agree to do – and, when he returns from receiving the sacrament and last rites of the Church, they take it in turns to clutch the crucifix which Priesthood has given him. Strength, Beauty, Discretion and Five Wits join Everyman in his last journey, only to desert him as they near its end – and even Knowledge is unable to go with him to his death. Good Deeds alone accompanies Everyman to his grave – whence an Angel joyfully summons his soul to Heaven. A Doctor instructs the audience in the moral of the play.

Characteristics of the Morality Plays

Both on its title page and in the printer's 'colophon', or tailpiece, to the book, *Everyman* is described as a 'moral play', but it was not until 1741 that the term 'morality' came into use to characterise the group of late medieval and early

modern plays which employ personifications to act out
allegories of man's spiritual progress on his journey from
birth to death and beyond. However, the description of
Everyman in one paperback guide, widely used by students,
as the 'most typical' of these 'moralities' is misleading, for
the play is really quite untypical of its kind. Firstly, it is
concerned with how Everyman, *already* a sinner, becomes
reconciled to the immediacy of death, rather than with the
struggle between forces of good and evil to gain control of
his life – such as takes place, for example, in the slightly
earlier (and also archetypally named) *Mankind*. Secondly,
instead of the ribald comedy and calculated variation in
tone that characterises *Mankind*, there is a throughline of
undeviating seriousness, from God's initial decision to call
Everyman to account right through to his final, literal ascent
as a repentant sinner into Heaven.

Not, perhaps, that any of the so-called moralities can be
called typical of this retrospectively defined genre. Of the
eight which their leading historian, Robert Potter, regards as
'repentance dramas', and which seem distinctively medieval
in their sensibility and themes, the earliest, the fragmentary
Pride of Life, dates from as early as the mid-fourteenth century,
and may be Irish in origin. In its staging requirements it
is evidently an ambitious piece – as also is *The Castle of
Perseverance*, of the early fifteenth century, whose manuscript
text includes an instructive layout for in-the-round performance. Here, the 'castle' of the title is at the centre of an
amphitheatre, surrounded by a neutral playing space, or
platea, with five scaffolds erected around the perimeter –
the 'mansions' or *sedes* which signified specific locations
or purposes.

From later in the fifteenth century came *Mankind*, with its rough-and-readier reverence apparently calculated to appeal to such audiences as might be assembled by a troupe of strolling players in a village square or before a market cross; and *Wisdom*, a piece evidently intended for a more sophisticated, probably urban audience, and perhaps originating from the Inns of Court in London. Of the pieces written, like *Everyman*, early in the sixteenth century, *Mundus et Infans* also seems designed for a travelling company, being small in scale though large in scope as it traces the transitions of the seven ages of man. *Hickscorner* is full of topical references to contemporary London and, like *Youth*, is concerned with the temptations of the town, which are displayed with some relish before being properly repudiated. Even among this group of its closest contemporaries, *Everyman* is clearly the *least* typical.

Whether 'of epic proportions' or 'rustic in their simplicity', the moralities are well summed up by Potter as 'intended to catch the conscience of a medieval audience . . . In style, they are presentational; in setting, they are microcosmic analogies' – a concept I discuss on page xvi – and 'in the originating circumstances of their performance, they are communal calls to repentance.'

Theological and Dramatic Form

If there are no good and bad angels contending in *Everyman* for the soul of a man – such as Marlowe was still using almost a century later in *Doctor Faustus* – the conflict is still between these opposing forces, at a yet more abstract level. The play conducts its exploration of what constitutes goodness against the received knowledge of man's fallen state, showing how Everyman's good works, mediated through knowledge, can only contribute to his salvation once he has undergone a theologically ordained process of contrition, confession, penance and absolution.

Some scholars have suggested that the figure in the play called Knowledge should truly be understood as representing what we would rather call 'Acknowledgement' – that is, the capacity for recognition of and repentance for his sins which Everyman duly shows. However, to the late medieval mind the concept of 'knowledge' would not have carried its modern sense – of accumulated data analytically processed – but, precisely, a full awareness of man's place in the divine plan, and of how to live and die in that conviction. That is what Everyman finally achieves.

Structurally and spiritually (as also in terms of playing time), the play divides almost exactly into two halves at line 463, with Everyman's long soliloquy beginning, 'O, to whom shall I make my moan', between his final desertion by Goods and his appeal to Good Deeds. For Everyman is deserted twice over: as John Conley puts it, he is first made bereft of 'goods of fortune', external to himself, and subsequently of 'goods of the soul', the qualities intrinsic to his very being, yet which haplessly also desert him at the last.

It is perhaps this process of remorseless stripping-away, first of worldly goods and then of physical attributes, which has led some critics to see the play, both unhistorically and untheologically, as tending towards tragedy. Yet it is understandable that *Everyman* should appear tragic to the modern mind – for even those qualities by which Everyman appears to rise above the temptations of the world and the flesh are shown in the end to be transient, and the isolation of death remains the ultimate reality to be confronted. Is not Good Deeds, the only comfort for Everyman in the grave, in this sense merely emblematic of all his illusory relationships with the world?

Yet for the play's first audiences the only possible tragedy was that of eternal damnation. And since Everyman is redeemed from that awful prospect, the play might more properly be termed, in the medieval sense, a comedy – such as was also enacted in the great fourteenth-century epic, the *Divine Comedy* of Dante. The critic Wilson Knight, in a characteristically eccentric insight, pointed out closer analogies – that Knowledge, 'who corresponds to Dante's Virgil, stays to the last to assure his safety; but only Good Deeds actually goes with him, like Dante's Beatrice, to paradise'. That Dante's heretical views of the Church led him, in the end, by the same path and to the same conclusion as the thoroughly orthodox author of *Everyman* affirms that for the medieval mind the achievement of paradise was the only needful aim.

As Raymond Williams sums up: 'Our approach to a play like *Everyman* is then not to a specimen of a primitive dramatic mode; but, rather, to recognition of a highly developed kind of drama, in which there is an organic connection between dramatic feeling and dramatic method. While the structure of feeling held, this kind of drama was not a forerunner, but was already mature.' It is, indeed, the 'structure of feeling' which we need to understand if we are to appreciate the appeal of plays that transcend both classical and modern concepts of dramatic form.

From Mysteries and Moralities to the Tudor Interlude

The later morality plays, such as came from the press of John Rastell, begin to show a humanist concern with the problems of how to live in this world rather than of how to prepare for the next. Even in this change of emphasis, they sit aptly enough alongside such moralities as *Everyman* in the early Tudor period – for this was theatrically as well as socially and politically a time of transition. The accession of the first Tudor monarch, Henry VII, in 1485 is no longer represented by historians as a sort of pivot between the medieval and early modern worlds: but his reign did see an uneasy overlap between them, as decaying feudal values contended uneasily with ill-understood forces of emergent capitalism. Such forces lie deep in the subtext which separates the spiritual values of *Everyman* from, say, those of Skelton's *Magnificence*, a product of tensions in the pre-Reformation court of Henry VIII.

The 'evolutionary' model for the development of medieval drama, for which Darwin gave nineteenth-century scholars so abiding a taste, is now discredited. The morality plays did not 'develop' from the mystery cycles any more than did the latter from 'liturgical dramas' – those quasi-theatrical interpolations into the mass, associated especially with Easter-tide, which began to appear as early as the tenth century. For the mystery plays, such as those that survive from York and Chester, were essentially civic celebrations, in which the urban craft guilds (or 'mysteries') lavished their wealth on the acting out of an episodic sequence of Bible stories.

Usually (though not invariably) the plays in these 'mystery cycles' were performed on pageant wagons dragged from station to station through the narrow streets of medieval cities. As the wagons halted at each prescribed viewing place on the processional route, members of the various guilds – carpenters, nailmakers, fishmongers, and so on – would perform there the play allotted to them, before trundling on to the next 'station'. And the mystery cycles went trundling on until late in the sixteenth century – when, so far from suffering any diminution in popularity, they were censored out of existence by the authorities for their associations with the old, Catholic theology whence they sprang (and whose repudiated feast, of Corpus Christi, they usually celebrated).

So the mysteries were not somehow 'displaced' by the morality tradition. Rather, the moralities developed and continued to flourish alongside – but they were, confessedly, better able to adapt to (as also to agitate for or against) the changing theological imperatives of the English Reformation. Besides, not only were the mystery cycles once-a-year celebrations, they were also (despite the hiring of professional aid for specialist purposes) essentially amateur – whereas the moralities were more closely linked with the emergence of a professional theatre, whose repertoire of 'interludes', embracing both sacred and secular offerings, was available for performance whenever and wherever an audience could be mustered.

Although Rastell is said to have erected a permanent stage in London in the 1520s, most such 'interludes' were still staged in 'found' environments, whether a churchyard, rough planks on barrels in a market-place, the enclosed yard of a galleried inn, the great hall of a nobleman's home – or the simple circle cleared amidst an open-air audience by an itinerant troupe. And it is of the essence of most Tudor interludes that they were readily adaptable to any or all of these circumstances.

The Original Staging of the Play

At around a thousand lines, *Everyman* is very similar in length to others of its kind – suggesting that, diverse though the occasions of interlude performance were, an hour or so of playing time met most needs. Indeed, the play's effective division into two halves, besides serving its theological purpose, allows an 'interval' at this point, whether for a new course to be served at a banqueting table or for a 'bottler' to beg for halfpennies in the market square. The break is also functional logistically – enabling the characters who disappear during the first half to be doubled with those who arrive only in the second, so that the parts can be shared out between a company of ten.

While props would almost certainly have been limited to the few made requisite by the text, the costuming would probably have been richer, and more emblematic – purposefully illustrative of the play's abstract roles (most notably in the case of Death, as discussed below). But displays of cavorting Deadly Sins (with which Marlowe was still enlivening *Doctor Faustus*) have no place here. And so, despite Everyman's presumed complicity with Fellowship when they were wont to 'haunt to women the lusty company' (line 273), lechery is notably absent from *Everyman*. But this is not to say that the play lacks references to gender: for while Fellowship and his ilk, like most of Everyman's personal attributes, are clearly masculine, both Good Deeds and Knowledge are women. The sudden affirmation of the latter's first appearance – 'Everyman, I will go with thee and be thy guide, / In thy most need to go by thy side' – must have been all the more resonant for the distinctive timbre of the boy player or chorister who would have spoken the lines (for no actresses

were to be allowed on an English stage for another hundred
and fifty years).

Just as the abstraction of character into moral quality or
physical attribute in *Everyman* is humanised by the actors'
presence, so (within the conventions of the early Tudor
drama) the play's sense of spatial relations is at once symbolic yet precise. There must, of course, be a scaffold raised
for Heaven, from which God can consider his fallen creation,
and to which Everyman may be summoned by the Angel at
the play's end – a location above the screen perhaps serving
the same purpose for an indoor performance at the far end
of a great hall. Surrounding this designated *locus* is the *platea* –
the 'place', or generalised playing area, here representing the
world.

Interestingly, God's long opening soliloquy deals almost
interchangeably with 'every man' in his plurality – perhaps
indicating the actors gathered in the 'place' beneath – and
Everyman in the singular: the particular person to be singled
out for instruction by Death. Indeed, he and some of the
other worldly characters may have made their entrances
from among the ordinary folk sitting around the playing
area – of whom they were, after all, both dramatically and
theologically representative.

Everyman's appeal to God 'in the high seat celestial' is, then,
literal, as is the immobility of Goods and Good Deeds, who
would appear to have required separate *loci*, suggestive of
their different kinds of physical confinement. Indeed, the
making appropriately burdensome of Goods has both a comic
and horrific potential – his inertia contrasting with the free-
dom of movement of those who hasten to excuse themselves

from proximity with the dying Everyman as they hasten off, perhaps out of sight behind the screen, perhaps merging into the outdoor audience whence they came.

Everyman receives the last sacraments offstage, presumably to avoid any suggestion of blasphemy (though 'boy bishops' were still conducting their 'sacred travesties' of the holiest office upon the Festival of Holy Innocents in cathedrals throughout the land). In regard to this, Raymond Williams argues for a 'lower room' in the scaffold on which Heaven is raised, to represent the terrestrial church – the 'House of Salvation' from which Confession can emerge, and into which Everyman can depart, both when he receives extreme unction and later to his grave. The Angel who summons the redeemed Everyman thence turns at the end to address the audience – just as God had embraced his wider creation at the start of the play. This opening and concluding gesture of inclusiveness is sustained by the Doctor who brings the action to a close. In his affirmation of the healing of Everyman's wound from Death's dart, the Doctor is close kin to his namesake in the mumming plays, who heals the 'deep and deadly wound' inflicted on St George – an unexpected 'correspondence', in the sense discussed in the following section, between the cultures of Christianity and the folk.

'Correspondences' and Kinds of Allegory

The theology of *Everyman* is both simple and subtle – simple in its total acceptance through symbolic enactment of the orthodoxies of the late-medieval Church, subtle in its network of allusions to biblical sources and the no-less revered writings of the early fathers of the Church. For the medieval mind loved and sought for 'correspondences' – exemplary connections between past and present, Old Testament and New, the wider 'macrocosm' (the greater or universal world) and the inner world at the 'microcosmic' level. Such correspondences could work in relation to events, people, or even objects: for instance, not only was Isaac perceived as prefiguring Jesus, but the tree of knowledge in the Garden of Eden as prefiguring the cross.

Those who relish complexity may share the pleasure taken by the medieval mind in teasing out the four possible levels at which correspondence could work. Of these, *analogy* (often generalised to embrace all kinds of correspondence in today's usage) in medieval terms represented only the level immediately beyond the literal – relating that first level to its reflection of the realised Christian inheritance. A further, *tropological* level was that of the individual soul, while the *anagogical* level represented the broader scheme of sacred or universal history. Thus, in the example here employed by Chris Baldick: 'Jerusalem is literally a city, allegorically the Church, tropologically the soul of the believer, and anagogically the heavenly City of God.' In this sense, the rambling, episodic 'mystery cycles' differ only in approach, not in subject, from such concise 'moralities' as *Everyman* – for while the former deal with the fall, redemption and last judgement of mankind throughout and beyond historical time, thus working both literally and by analogy, *Everyman* enacts corresponding events in tropologic and anagogic terms.

Such niceties would not, however, have been uppermost in the minds of most audiences of *Everyman*, however pious. For medieval Christianity, though pervasive, was a *mediated* religion – the interpretation of its scriptures and the making of its doctrine a jealously guarded prerogative of the Church. Even the reading of the scriptures by the laity was actively discouraged, and it is no accident that the first translator of the Bible into English, in the late fourteenth century, was the 'heretical' John Wycliffe. It took the Reformation to put a vernacular translation of the Bible within reach of ordinary people, and even then the limited extent of literacy meant that relatively few could read it for themselves. Until that time, morality plays, along with the sermons with which the new orders of mendicant (or begging) friars had familiarised the population, were rather modes of instruction than for disputing interpretation.

Literacy, of course, was needed also to set plays down in writing – and since setting anything down in writing was largely the preserve of the clerical classes, we should not be surprised that so much of surviving medieval drama is concerned with the Christian religion. For clerics took notice of secular playing only when it offended the dignity of the Church or themselves – and were certainly not interested in recording its impieties and recurrent strain of anti-clericalism for posterity. Besides, so much of medieval life was rooted in the religious impulse (even when in tension with its urgings) that the extant drama may not be so very unrepresentative.

The Sources and Shaping of Everyman

Everyman reflects theological concerns both specific to its own time and as old as Christianity itself. The main 'live issues' touched on are the propriety of pilgrimages and the value of confessing one's sins to a priest – the play in both cases duly proselytising for the orthodox position of the Church. (The same themes had earlier been debated in the Croxton *Play of the Sacraments* of *c.* 1460, under the guise of dramatising the story of Jews converted by the miraculous powers of the Host.) The play has also been seen as a topical reflection of the reformist movement which went under the name 'devotio moderna': this had originated, like *Everyman*, in the Netherlands, but it prioritised personal devotion and Christian conduct over the external observances – mediated through the priesthood – which *Everyman* seems concerned to promote.

Such issues are marginal to the play's dominant themes – an assertion of the worthlessness of worldly things in the face of death, and of the need to make one's own death a preparation for life everlasting. The oldest of the Christian sources suggested for the play (aside from the Bible itself) is the *Psychomachia* of the fourth-century Christian poet Prudentius: but this should more accurately be regarded as an antecedent of such moralities as *Mankind*, anticipating as it does the struggle between good and evil over the soul of a man tempted by all the pleasures of life before being nudged towards repentance. In *Everyman*, as we have seen, that struggle is already over.

Rather, the play reworks in its own terms the traditional fable of faithless friendship which took perhaps its earliest form in the seventh-century *Barlaam and Josaphat*. Conflated with this is the concern so characteristic of the late Middle Ages with the imminence of death – a concern which found widespread earlier expression, and of which the most popular contemporary account was translated into English and printed by Caxton in 1490 as *The Book of the Craft of Dying*. In 1507 a similar work from the press of Caxton's successor, Wynkyn de Worde, actually took dialogue form. Although

printing was itself one of the harbingers of a world in which
living might again appear more important than dying, the
craft at its birth thus gave even wider currency to the belief
that only through constant reminders of death – or *memento
mori* – could a life so generally nasty, brutish and short be
made more tolerable.

In Remembrance of Death

The Middle Ages contemplated death from three directions –
looking soberly backwards, at the transitory glory of fallen
empires and of emperors turned to dust; reflecting in the
present how suddenly and unexpectedly Death may choose
his moment; and anticipating what the future will inevitably
bring – the decay of physical beauty, the decomposition of
the body after death, and its final release from the grave to
receive God's terrible judgement.

For well over a century before the writing of *Everyman*,
contemplation of physical decay had been the dominant
perspective, and there was widespread trepidation that the
world was nearing its long-predicted end. Recurrent famines
and climatic disasters in the early fourteenth century had
left a population ill-fitted to resist the cataclysm of the Black
Death in the late 1340s, and in the intervening years the
plague had become endemic (if slightly less virulent) throughout Europe. The resulting shortage of labour had a little
bettered the bargaining position of the poor, but had led also
to a breakdown of old feudal certainties as the privileged elite
showed its ruthlessness in suppressing popular uprisings such
as the Peasants' Revolt of 1381.

Since 1338, England had been pursuing the claim to the French throne which gave rise to the so-called 'Hundred Years War'. This in fact dragged on intermittently until 1453, by which time early English victories had so far been reversed as to leave only the barest toehold in Calais – with anarchy now threatening at home, as the nobility fought out the spasmodic civil battles of the Wars of the Roses. By the turn of the century, when *Everyman* was being performed, it was far too early to be confident that the victory of Henry Tudor at the Battle of Bosworth had resolved the issue.

Although such campaigns had less impact on the lives of ordinary people than one would guess from political histories (or from the chronicle plays of Shakespeare), they were conducted with a disregard for human life which, four centuries earlier, would have been unthinkable to a Charlemagne or an Alfred the Great, supposedly struggling out of the 'barbarism' of the Dark Ages. Even so reputedly heroic and magnanimous a ruler as Henry V had, in 1418, refused to permit non-combatants from the Siege of Rouen to pass through his lines – watching impassively as 12,000 women, children and old men starved or froze to slow deaths before the walls of their own city.

When Henry V himself died during a later campaign in France, his bones were boiled away from his flesh in order that they might be transported back to England for interment. This common practice (for those who could afford it), resulted from a superstitious desire to be buried in one's native soil, and was typical of the age's obsession with the physical trappings of death – as evident also, for example, in the veneration of saint's bodies which had apparently remained uncorrupted in their tombs.

All this was reflected both in sacred and in popular art. Orcagna's great fresco, 'The Triumph of Death', painted immediately after the Black Death for the Church of Santa Croce in Florence, shows a royal hunting party coming upon a field of open graves, in which the rotting corpses also wear crowns; meanwhile, a clawed figure of Death hovers unnoticed over a party of feasting debauchees, but ignores the lepers and cripples who would welcome release from their suffering. As in *Everyman*, Death comes to those who are least expecting its visitation.

Later in the fourteenth century, the word *macabré* was coined in France to describe the novel conception of a 'dance of death' between the living and the dead. In some of these *danses macabres*, figures representing the various orders of society are shown being dragged to their graves by their own corpses. Originally, Death was represented simply as a skeletal corpse: later, personified as God's messenger, he often became an ironically egalitarian figure, destined to level in mortality all ranks and professions of men. (With more regard for 'correspondence' than equality, women were accorded a dance of their own.)

Possibly originating in performance, the Dance of Death has, of course, survived mainly through pictorial art, though the court poet John Lydgate wrote sets of verses as a commentary upon a Dance of Death which embellished the north cloister walls of Old St Paul's. The similar mural upon which members of fashionable society in Paris could gaze as they strolled among the charnel houses of the Church of Holy Innocents was reproduced in the woodcuts of the *Danse Macabre*, published by Guyot Marchant in 1485. The art of printing thus increased the accessibility of such images, and

Death with his dart duly appears on the title page of John Skot's editions of *Everyman*.

So Death in *Everyman* would have been a personification familiar to the play's original audiences. Yet the progress towards absolution he initiates in the play is necessary not because Everyman has lived his life with due regard for his mortality, but precisely because he has *failed* to do so – and in this the play again reflected a changing society. By the turn of the sixteenth century, worldly pleasures were becoming more accessible to all, and the promises of new discoveries and a New World were beginning to beckon – so maybe the cautionary presence of Death in *Everyman* is as much in consequence of a life now lived with greater relish as of the old obsession with the macabre. What appears to us an aspect of the acute morbidity of an earlier age may be, at least in part, an expression of a collective guilty conscience, induced by the enjoyment of better times.

Lollardy and the Rise of Anti-Clericalism

It was surely no coincidence that John Wycliffe, leader of the Lollard movement which anticipated by a century the protestant Reformation, was a member of that sceptical generation which grew up in the shadow of the Black Death. For the plague had exposed the weakness of the clergy on two counts: those priests who fled to supposed safety clearly forfeited the trust of their parishioners – while those who remained faithful to their flocks were among the likeliest to succumb, because of their concern for the dying and the dead, and so gave cause for doubt to a superstitious laity, surprised that God had failed to protect his own. Conversely, as the material expectations of labouring people increased, thanks to the shortage of labour and plenitude of land resulting from the plague, the nobility came increasingly to regard the Church as a last bulwark against egalitarian tendencies, increasing the popular perception of the Church as an institution which served the interests of the elite.

This perception was enhanced by the wealth of the Church itself. The representation of Everyman being weighed down by worldly goods in excess of his needs may have seemed ironic to many at a time when the Church was just as stifled (and often corrupted) by a wealth far in excess of the secular state's – making it, of course, all the riper for Henry VIII's imminent depredations. Thus, according to a Venetian envoy in 1497, monasteries were 'more like baronial palaces than religious houses'. And the age's obsession with death led to the widespread endowment of chantry chapels – often with a school attached to betoken 'good works', but primarily to enable the singing of masses for the souls of those whose excess of worldly goods, so far from weighing them down, had purchased them such posthumous indulgence.

If the influence of Lollardy as a movement was short-lived, the anti-clerical spirit it encouraged pervaded much of the polemical writing of the period. V.J. Scattergood, in his authoritative study of *Politics and Poetry in the Fifteenth Century*, declares that, despite some anti-Lollard ripostes, 'for the most part fifteenth-century poets concentrate on the perennial topics of the materialism, inefficiency and immorality of the Church and the clergy'. No wonder that Everyman's initial instinct is to see whether Death can be tempted with a monetary bribe. And no wonder that while he is receiving the last rites, Knowledge and Five Wits chat defensively about the *faults* as well as the virtues of the clergy. This, in the broader context of the play's religious orthodoxy, is presumably a pre-emptive tactic – an acknowledgement of a few 'bad eggs' (for such will surely be known to the audience), in the confidence that 'no such may we find'.

So *Everyman*, no less than the earlier moralities, is as much an assertion as an expression of the Church's authority. The need to impress the awfulness of death upon men's minds in part derived from the loosening of restraints upon earthly enjoyments and ambitions – a process that was, of course, to prove as irrevocable as the capitalist individualism it anticipated. And so, while the mind-set of the play may at first appear medieval, it is very much in touch with early-modern concerns – not least in its attempt to harmonise the traditional metaphor of the pilgrimage, as Everyman seeks for travellers to accompany him on his journey, with that of the rendering and settling of his account.

The Rendering of Everyman's Account

Everyman's book of accounts, which he has in his own possession, is not to be confused with the 'book of life' recording the names of the saved – which, according to the biblical Book of Revelations, is kept by God. Yet the importance attached to these personal 'accounts' by the play's contemporary audiences is evident from its title page – where we find *Everyman* described as a 'moral play' telling 'how the High Father of Heaven sendeth Death to summon every creature to come and give account of their lives in this world'. Of course, this may be the printer's rather than the author's emphasis – but it is none the less significant in its reflection of what was considered the play's overriding concern. Indeed, the emphasis is recurrent throughout the play proper: the medievalist V.A. Kolve has enumerated no fewer than 25 occasions on which forms of 'account' and 'reckoning' occur, 'always at moments of high urgency, where most meaning is being gathered in fewest words'.

The lack of versions of the Bible in their own language (not actually prohibited, though widely believed to be so) meant that the English were probably less well acquainted with the scriptures than any other nation in Europe – except, of course, as interpreted to them through sermons, or through such rough 'translations' as the mystery cycles. This calls in doubt Kolve's suggestion that it is the parable of the talents that is being invoked by the recurrent references to rendering an account of God's loan – for if the author of *Everyman* had intended such a reference, 'talent' is surely the term he would have used. There seems no need to understand Everyman's book of accounts other than as precisely that: a return rendered to God of the use made of his capital investment.

Certainly, emergent capitalist individualism was encouraging the understanding of human needs and impulses in just such transactional terms. Shakespeare puts this gloss on the medieval concept of 'honour' when, in *Henry V*, he has Prince Hal declare that he intends his rival Percy to 'engross up glorious deeds' on his behalf: whereupon, 'I will call him to so strict account / That he shall render every glory up . . . / Or I will tear the reckoning from his heart'. Even in the lives of those supposedly most detached from economic concerns, good works were becoming no less regarded as negotiable currency: thus, the renowned fifteenth-century mystic Margery Kempe made dispositions of the 'surplus' of good works she felt she had accumulated, and so might transfer for the benefit of other people's souls. The less generous, of course, wanted all their good works credited to their own account – as in the case of Henry VII, who left funds in his will of 1509 for the celebration of ten thousand masses to be said for his soul, at the generous rate of sixpence apiece.

Everyman remains sufficiently a medieval play that the 'correspondence' of Everyman's life with that of his saviour requires him to undergo the penance of scourging before the crippled Good Deeds can be made whole. Only then can Knowledge clothe Everyman with the garment of penitence, and the book of reckoning become clear – or, at the level of the mercantile metaphor, the balance be reconciled. I can't help but be reminded, at one extreme, of those Chinese emperors who were entombed not only with simulacra of their worldly goods, but with their accounts made up ready for presentation to the Lord of Heaven – and, at the other, of my own monthly struggle with pocket calculator, bank statement, and cheque stubs to achieve a late-capitalist 'reconciliation'.

The Language and Versification

Barely a century before the performance of *Everyman*, in 1390, John Gower had been among the earliest poets to write a substantial work of literature in Middle English. Yet Gower gave his poem a Latin title, the *Confessio Amantis*, and wrote other works in that tongue – and Latin had, of course, long been the *lingua franca* for diplomatic, ecclesiastical, and administrative purposes. Gower wrote also in French, which since the Norman invasion had been the language of the social elite – although it was his near contemporary Chaucer who was the first to make the vernacular the language of literary choice. While the ensuing century produced relatively little of conventional literary merit, it did see the consolidation of English as a national language. It also saw the transition from the various dialects of Middle English to an increasingly standardised form – and in *Everyman* (unlike, say, the earlier mystery plays) that form is recognisably 'modern'.

Simply regularising the play's spelling, as in this edition, is sufficient in the way of updating to impress us with the play's directness and simplicity of expression. Contemporary audiences might have been surprised by this directness: they were probably more accustomed at one extreme to the ornate Latinisms of the so-called 'aureate style', and at the other to the sort of streetwise colloquialisms which often (for a modern reader) end up being no less obscure. *Mankind* used both, in the interests of its wider range of characterisation: but *Everyman* prefers a sustained neutrality of language as of tone, making it both a less vivid and a less varied piece than *Mankind*, but enabling it to sustain a clear rhetorical and theological throughline, focusing our attention on the matter rather than the manner of its presentation.

The Messenger's first speech has a strange but emphatic rhyming scheme – a succession of couplets, each followed by a third line whose rhyme completes that unit of thought yet is also carried through the whole speech. This pattern is easier to recognise than describe, and, once recognised, compels the actor's attentive response. Thereafter, the mixture of couplets and quatrains, in metres which vary functionally rather than schematically, keeps both actors and audience alert to the different kinds of emphasis and rhythms imposed.

Although these are sometimes for the convenience of the rhyme as much as for the rhetoric, there is an underlying complexity which makes the relative predictability of Elizabethan blank verse, varied by heroic couplets, seem almost formal by comparison. However, because for most English actors 'verse speaking' *means* the speaking of such rhymed or unrhymed iambic pentameters, the sheer freshness and difference of *Everyman* cannot but catch the actor's breath and present pause for thought. Indeed, one might say that thoughtful pausing is as much of the essence here as in any speech of Shakespeare's.

Everyman in the Twentieth Century

For almost four centuries after the Reformation *Everyman* dropped out of the living repertoire of the theatre, until William Poel brought the play back to life on the London stage in 1901. Poel was an experimental and often eccentric director whose Elizabethan Stage Society, active for a decade after its formation in 1895, set out to restore the plays of the Elizabethans to the conditions of their original staging – an aim in which his success is perhaps better measured in the less pedantically uncluttered approach of his follower, Granville Barker. Indeed, so accustomed was Poel to defending his ideas against critical derision that he seems almost to have been embarrassed by the success of his revival of *Everyman* – from which, as the evidence of the prompt books shows, he cut anything remotely controversial, in order to give the play, in Robert Potter's phrase, 'a more congenial pre-Raphaelite texture'. There appears to have been even more trimming in subsequent revivals (including a successful American tour),

for which Poel handed over responsibility to Ben Greet —
who was himself still playing the Doctor just a year before
his death as he neared the age of eighty in 1936.

Yeats and Shaw were among contemporary dramatists who
professed to have been influenced by Poel's production. Shaw
acknowledged that Ann Whitefield in *Man and Superman*
began for him as a female equivalent to Everyman — which
is helpful to understanding that curious interpolated playlet,
Don Juan in Hell, when Ann finally chooses Heaven over Hell,
rebirth over death. Shaw, of course, was proselytising for
his own quasi-religion of creative evolution rather than for
Christianity: more in tune with the original was the German
version, *Jedermann*, written in 1911 by Hugo von Hofmannsthal for the Austrian director Max Reinhardt. Reinhardt,
who had seen the Poel production, encouraged Hofmannsthal
to give the play a modern, materialist slant — as its subtitle,
'The Play of the Rich Man's Death', suggests.

A Mother, Mammon, and Mephistopheles appear in the cast
of this spectacular adaptation, which incorporated scenes
showing Everyman's earlier earthly life — including a banquet
from which he is summoned by the appearance of Death.
The piece became the inaugural production of the Salzburg
Festival in 1920 — the sunset over the city and the cathedral
bells being incorporated into its environmentalist setting.
It remained a regular feature of the festival, and a touring
production reached as far afield as Hollywood in 1935.

Allegorical figures featured also in Hofmannsthal's *Das Salz-
burger grosse Welttheater* (*The Salzburg Great Theatre of the World*),
inspired as much by the *danse macabre* as by Calderon, and
designed as a counterpart to *Jedermann*. While clearly indebted

to their medieval antecedents, such productions are also inextricably linked with (and fed into) the development of German expressionism. The often spectacular – though always integrally significant – scenography was, of course, Reinhardt's contribution: but the conflation of the symbolic and generalised with the realistic and particular is as evident in the medieval originals as in the work of Sternheim, Toller, or Kaiser – or, indeed, in the more recent recovery of the expressionist impulse in productions by Stephen Daldry, from Sophie Treadwell's *Machinal* and J.B. Priestley's *An Inspector Calls* to Arnold Wesker's *The Kitchen*.

An Inspector Calls, in particular, with its visitation of a family of sinners by an all-knowing being, has strong thematic as well as stylistic echoes of the morality tradition – as does Priestley's slightly earlier (and more overtly expressionistic) *Johnson over Jordon* (1943), whose central character, journeying towards his death, was even described by the dramatist as 'an English Everyman'. Sutton Vane's *Outward Bound* (1923) deployed the even older belief in a voyage across water towards death – the 'messenger', here a grizzled bar steward, a figure half way between Death in *Everyman* and Charon, the boatman of the mythical underworld. Ingmar Bergman created a more distinctly medieval visitant in *The Seventh Seal*, a play before it became a film, which even included a climactic 'dance' in its chill updating of the medieval obsession with death.

There is not only a proto-expressionism about *Everyman*, but a proto-absurdism besides. The images of humankind consigned to dustbins and wheelchairs in Beckett's *Endgame*, or half-buried in the earth like Winnie in *Happy Days*, are alike reminiscent of the initial paralysis of Good Deeds in *Everyman*.

The engulfing tide of replicating objects in, say, Ionesco's *The Chairs*, or the cloying threat of the barely animate, as embodied by the *schmürz* of Boris Vian's *The Empire Builders*, are similarly anticipated by Goods in *Everyman*, half-thing and half-human as the text reveals him.

Last Judgements

A significant cultural side-effect of the Poel production of *Everyman* was the creation in 1906 of that long-enduring series of pocket classics, accumulating to over a thousand volumes, named 'Everyman's Library' when its first editor, Ernest Rhys, recollected the lines that served for many years as an epigraph on the end-papers: 'Everyman, I will go with thee and be thy guide, / In thy most need to go by thy side.' The publisher of the series, J.M. Dent, claimed to have 'repaid something of the debt we owed to *Everyman*' when, in 1930, he commissioned Thomas Derrick to illustrate 'as lively a production of a play as is possible inside a book' with a sequence of seventy-three woodcuts. The artist's own verdict on the play was succinct: 'The play is not old. Neither is it new. It is true.'

Against this, we may set a criticism not specifically of *Everyman*, but of so much art in the death-obsessed fifteenth century, made by the Dutch historian Johan Huizinga in his now-classic work, *The Waning of the Middle Ages* (1924). There was, Huizinga suggests, an absence of expressed feeling between 'lamentation about the briefness of all earthly glory, and jubilation over the salvation of the soul. All that lay between – pity, resignation, longing, consolation – remained unexpressed and was, so to say, absorbed by the too much accentuated and too vivid representation of Death hideous and threatening. Living emotion stiffens amid the abused imagery of skeletons and worms.'

Perhaps there is a truth about *Everyman* lying somewhere in the tension between these two judgements.

Simon Trussler

For Further Reading

William Tydeman's *The Theatre in the Middle Ages* (Cambridge UP, 1978) is perhaps the best overview of the theatre of the later Middle Ages, at once scholarly and accessible, while David Bevington's *From Mankind to Marlowe* (Harvard University Press, 1962) is an admirable introduction to the transitional period before the great age of Elizabethan drama. *Medieval Drama*, by Christine Richardson and Jackie Johnson (Routledge, 1991), combines its conspective account with modern theoretical concerns. *Medieval English Drama: a Casebook*, ed. Peter Happé (Macmillan, 1984) and *Medieval Drama* in the 'Stratford-upon-Avon Studies' series (Arnold, 1973) provide a range of critical samplings. *The Cambridge Companion to Medieval English Theatre*, edited by Richard Beadle (Cambridge University Press, 1994), concisely surveys the present state of knowledge and critical opinion.

Robert Potter's *The English Morality Play* (Routledge, 1975) is a sound introduction both to the genre as such and to its cultural history. T.W. Craik's *The Tudor Interlude: Stage, Costume and Acting* (Leicester University Press, 1958) remains useful on methods of staging and acting conventions, which William Tydeman's *English Medieval Theatre*, in the 'Theatre Production Studies' series (Routledge, 1986) valuably illustrates in relation to specific plays.

Further examples of the type may be found in *English Moral Interludes*, ed. Glynne Wickham (Dent, 1976), and in the Penguin selection of *Tudor Interludes*, ed. Peter Happé (1972). For more detailed study and annotation of *Everyman* itself, our own copy text is included with two other moralities in *Three Late Medieval Morality Plays*, edited by G.A. Lester for the 'New Mermaids' series. A.C. Cawley's *Everyman* (Manchester University Press, 1961) remains an excellent old-spelling edition, and may be easier to obtain than the more recent (and critically more incisive) edition by Christopher Wortham and Geoffrey Cooper for the University of Western Australia Press.

Everyman: Key Dates

1376   First mention of York mystery cycle.

1400   *c. The Castle of Perseverance.*

1422   First mention of Chester mystery cycle.

1465   *c. Mankind.*

1476   Caxton sets up first printing press in England.

1485   Battle of Bosworth and accession of Henry VII.

1492   Columbus's 'discovery' of the New World.

1495   *c.* Dutch play of *Elckerlijc.*

1500   *c.* English version of *Everyman.*

1509   Accession of Henry VIII.

1513-14 *Youth* and *Hickscorner.*

1522   Skelton's *Magnificence.*

1531   Henry VIII breaks with Rome: beginnings of English Reformation.

1901   Poel's production of *Everyman*, the first recorded since the Reformation.

EVERYMAN

Dramatis Personae

MESSENGER
GOD
DEATH
EVERYMAN
FELLOWSHIP
KINDRED
COUSIN
GOODS
GOOD DEEDS
KNOWLEDGE
CONFESSION
BEAUTY
STRENGTH
DISCRETION
FIVE WITS
ANGEL
DOCTOR

Here beginneth a treatise how the High Father of Heaven sendeth death to summon every creature to come and give account of their lives in this world, and is in manner of a moral play.

MESSENGER.

I pray you all give your audience
And hear this matter with reverence,
By figure a moral play!
The Summoning of Everyman called it is,
That of our lives and ending shows   5
How transitory we be all day.
This matter is wondrous precious,
But the intent of it is more gracious
And sweet to bear away.
The story saith: Man, in the beginning   10
Look well, and take good heed to the ending,
Be you never so gay!
Ye think sin in the beginning full sweet,
Which in the end causeth the soul to weep,
When the body lieth in clay.   15
Here shall you see how Fellowship and Jollity,
Both Strength, Pleasure, and Beauty
Will fade from thee as flower in May;
For ye shall hear how our Heaven King
Calleth every man to a general reckoning.   20
Give audience, and hear what he doth say!

[*Exit* MESSENGER.]

GOD *speaketh.*

GOD.
  I perceive, here in my majesty,
  How that all creatures be to me unkind,
  Living without dread in worldly prosperity.
  Of ghostly sight the people be so blind;   25
  Drowned in sin, they know me not for their God.
  In worldly riches is all their mind;
  They fear not my righteousness, the sharp rod.
  My law, that I showed when I for them died,
  They forget clean, and shedding of my blood red.   30
  I hanged between two thieves, it cannot be denied;
  To get them life I suffered to be dead.
  I healed their feet; with thorns hurt was my head.
  I could do no more than I did, truly.
  And now I see the people do clean forsake me.   35
  They use the seven deadly sins damnable,
  As pride, covetise, wrath, and lechery
  Now in the world be made commendable.
  And thus they leave of angels the heavenly company.
  Every man liveth so after his own pleasure,   40
  And yet of their life they be nothing sure.
  I see the more that I them forbear
  The worse they be fro year to year.
  All that liveth appaireth fast;
  Therefore I will, in all the haste,   45
  Have a reckoning of every man's person.
  For, and I leave the people thus alone
  In their life and wicked tempests,

Verily they will become much worse than beasts.
For now one would by envy another up eat;   50
Charity they do all clean forget.
I hoped well that every man
In my glory should make his mansion,
And thereto I had them all elect;
But now I see, like traitors deject,   55
They thank me not for the pleasure that I to them meant,
Nor yet for their being that I them have lent.
I proffered the people great multitude of mercy,
And few there be that asketh it heartily.
They be so cumbered with worldly riches   60
That needs on them I must do justice,
On every man living without fear.
Where art thou, Death, thou mighty messenger?

[*Enter* DEATH.]

DEATH.

Almighty God, I am here at your will,
Your commandment to fulfil.   65

GOD.

Go thou to Everyman
And show him, in my name,
A pilgrimage he must on him take,
Which he in no wise may escape,
And that he bring with him a sure reckoning   70
Without delay or any tarrying.

DEATH.

Lord, I will in the world go run over all

And cruelly outsearch both great and small.
Every man will I beset that liveth beastly,
Out of God's laws, and dreadeth not folly.   75
He that loveth richesse I will strike with my dart,
His sight to blind, and fro heaven to depart,
Except that Alms be his good friend,
In hell for to dwell, world without end.

[GOD *retires. Enter* EVERYMAN, *finely dressed.*]

Lo, yonder I see Everyman walking;   80
Full little he thinketh on my coming.
His mind is on fleshly lusts and his treasure,
And great pain it shall cause him to endure
Before the Lord, Heaven King.

[*Touches* EVERYMAN *with his dart.*]

Everyman, stand still! Whither art thou going   85
Thus gaily? Hast thou thy maker forget?

EVERYMAN.
    Why askest thou?
    Wouldest thou wit?

DEATH.
    Yea, sir, I will show you.
    In great haste I am sent to thee   90
    Fro God, out of his majesty.

EVERYMAN.
    What, sent to me?

DEATH.
Yea, certainly.
Though thou have forget him here,
He thinketh on thee in the heavenly sphere,   95
As, ere we depart, thou shalt know.

EVERYMAN.
What desireth God of me?

DEATH.
That shall I show thee.
A reckoning he will needs have,
Without any longer respite.   100

EVERYMAN.
To give a reckoning longer leisure I crave.
This blind matter troubleth my wit.

DEATH.
On thee thou must take a long journey;
Therefore thy book of count with thee thou bring,
For turn again thou cannot by no way.   105
And look thou be sure of thy reckoning,
For before God thou shalt answer and show
Thy many bad deeds, and good but a few,
How thou hast spent thy life, and in what wise,
Before the chief Lord of paradise.   110
Have ado that we were in that way,
For, wit thou well, thou shalt make none attorney.

EVERYMAN.
Full unready I am such reckoning to give.
I know thee not. What messenger art thou?

DEATH.

    I am Death, that no man dreadeth,   115

    For every man I rest, and no man spareth,

    For it is God's commandment

    That all to me should be obedient.

EVERYMAN.

    O Death, thou comest when I had thee least in mind!

    In thy power it lieth me to save.   120

    Yet of my good will I give thee, if thou will be kind –

    Yea, a thousand pound shalt thou have,

    And defer this matter till another day.

DEATH.

    Everyman, it may not be, by no way.

    I set not by gold, silver, nor richesse,   125

    Ne by pope, emperor, king, duke, ne princess.

    For, and I would receive gifts great,

    All the world I might get.

    But my custom is clean contrary.

    I give thee no respite. Come hence, and not tarry.   130

EVERYMAN.

    Alas, shall I have no longer respite?

    I may say, 'Death giveth no warning!'

    To think on thee it maketh my heart sick,

    For all unready is my book of reckoning.

    But twelve year and I might have abiding,   135

    My counting-book I would make so clear

    That my reckoning I should not need to fear.

    Wherefore, Death, I pray thee, for God's mercy,

    Spare me till I be provided of remedy.

DEATH.

    Thee availeth not to cry, weep, and pray;   140
    But haste thee lightly that thou were gone that journey,
    And prove thy friends if thou can,
    For, wit thou well, the tide abideth no man,
    And in the world each living creature
    For Adam's sin must die of nature.   145

EVERYMAN.

    Death, if I should this pilgrimage take,
    And my reckoning surely make,
    Show me, for saint charity,
    Should I not come again shortly?

DEATH.

    No, Everyman; and thou be once there,   150
    Thou mayst never more come here,
    Trust me verily.

EVERYMAN.

    O gracious God in the high seat celestial,
    Have mercy on me in this most need!
    Shall I have no company fro this vale terrestrial   155
    Of mine acquaintance, that way me to lead?

DEATH.

    Yea, if any be so hardy
    That would go with thee and bear thee company.
    Hie thee that thou were gone to God's magnificence,
    Thy reckoning to give before his presence.   160
    What, weenest thou thy life is given thee?
    And thy worldly goods also?

EVERYMAN.
I had wend so, verily.

DEATH.
Nay, nay, it was but lent thee.
For, as soon as thou art go,   165
Another a while shall have it, and then go therefro,
Even as thou hast done.
Everyman, thou art mad. Thou hast thy wits five
And here on earth will not amend thy life,
For suddenly I do come.   170

EVERYMAN.
O wretched caitiff, whither shall I flee,
That I might scape this endless sorrow?
Now, gentle Death, spare me till tomorrow,
That I may amend me
With good advisement.   175

DEATH.
Nay, thereto I will not consent,
Nor no man will I respite;
But to the heart suddenly I shall smite
Without any advisement.
And now out of thy sight I will me hie.   180
See thou make thee ready shortly,
For thou mayst say this is the day
That no man living may scape away.

[*Exit* DEATH.]

EVERYMAN.

Alas, I may well weep with sighs deep!
Now have I no manner of company   185
To help me in my journey, and me to keep,
And also my writing is full unready.
How shall I do now for to excuse me?
I would to God I had never be get!
To my soul a full great profit it had be,   190
For now I fear pains huge and great.
The time passeth. Lord, help, that all wrought!
For though I mourn it availeth nought.
The day passeth and is almost ago.
I wot not well what for to do.   195
To whom were I best my complaint to make?
What and I to Fellowship thereof spake,
And showed him of this sudden chance?
For in him is all mine affiance.
We have in the world so many a day   200
Be good friends in sport and play.

[*Enter* FELLOWSHIP, *at a distance.*]

I see him yonder, certainly!
I trust that he will bear me company;
Therefore to him will I speak to ease my sorrow.
Well met, good Fellowship, and good morrow!   205

FELLOWSHIP *speaketh.*

FELLOWSHIP.

Everyman, good morrow, by this day!
Sir, why lookest thou so piteously?

If anything be amiss, I pray thee me say,
That I may help to remedy.

EVERYMAN.
Yea, good Fellowship, yea.   210
I am in great jeopardy.

FELLOWSHIP.
My true friend, show to me your mind.
I will not forsake thee to my life's end,
In the way of good company.

EVERYMAN.
That was well spoken, and lovingly.   215

FELLOWSHIP.
Sir, I must needs know your heaviness;
I have pity to see you in any distress.
If any have you wronged, ye shall revenged be,
Though I on the ground be slain for thee,
Though that I know before that I should die.   220

EVERYMAN.
Verily, Fellowship, gramercy.

FELLOWSHIP.
Tush, by thy thanks I set not a straw!
Show me your grief, and say no more.

EVERYMAN.
If I my heart should to you break,
And then you to turn your mind fro me   225

And would not me comfort when ye hear me speak,
Then should I ten times sorrier be.

FELLOWSHIP.
   Sir, I say as I will do, indeed!

EVERYMAN.
   Then be you a good friend at need!
   I have found you true herebefore.   230

FELLOWSHIP.
   And so ye shall evermore,
   For, in faith, and thou go to hell,
   I will not forsake thee by the way.

EVERYMAN.
   Ye speak like a good friend; I believe you well.
   I shall deserve it, and I may.   235

FELLOWSHIP.
   I speak of no deserving, by this day!
   For he that will say, and nothing do,
   Is not worthy with good company to go.
   Therefore show me the grief of your mind,
   As to your friend most loving and kind.   240

EVERYMAN.
   I shall show you how it is:
   Commanded I am to go a journey,
   A long way, hard and dangerous,
   And give a strait count, without delay,
   Before the high Judge, Adonai.   245

Wherefore, I pray you, bear me company,
As ye have promised, in this journey.

FELLOWSHIP.
That is matter indeed! Promise is duty,
But, and I should take such a voyage on me,
I know it well it should be to my pain.   250
Also it maketh me afeard, certain.
But let us take counsel here as well as we can,
For your words would fear a strong man.

EVERYMAN.
Why, ye said if I had need
Ye would me never forsake, quick ne dead,   255
Though it were to hell, truly!

FELLOWSHIP.
So I said, certainly;
But such pleasures be set aside, the sooth to say;
And also, if we took such a journey,
When should we again come?   260

EVERYMAN.
Nay, never again, till the day of doom.

FELLOWSHIP.
In faith, then will not I come there!
Who hath you these tidings brought?

EVERYMAN.
Indeed, Death was with me here.

FELLOWSHIP.

Now, by God that all hath bought,   265
If Death were the messenger,
For no man that is living today
I will not go that loath journey!
Not for the father that begat me!

EVERYMAN.

Ye promised otherwise, pardie!   270

FELLOWSHIP.

I wot well I said so, truly.
And yet, if thou wilt eat, and drink, and make good cheer,
Or haunt to women the lusty company,
I would not forsake you while the day is clear,
Trust me verily.   275

EVERYMAN.

Yea, thereto ye would be ready!
To go to mirth, solace, and play
Your mind will sooner apply
Than to bear me company in my long journey.

FELLOWSHIP.

Now, in good faith, I will not that way.   280
But, and thou will murder, or any man kill –
In that I will help thee with a good will.

EVERYMAN.

O, that is a simple advice indeed!
Gentle fellow, help me in my necessity.

We have loved long, and now I need;   285
And now, gentle Fellowship, remember me.

FELLOWSHIP.

Whether ye have loved me or no,
By Saint John, I will not with thee go.

EVERYMAN.

Yet, I pray thee, take the labour and do so much for me
To bring me forward, for saint charity,   290
And comfort me till I come without the town.

FELLOWSHIP.

Nay, and thou would give me a new gown,
I will not a foot with thee go;
But, and thou had tarried, I would not have left thee so.
And, as now, God speed thee in thy journey,   295
For from thee I will depart as fast as I may.

EVERYMAN.

Whither away, Fellowship? Will thou forsake me?

FELLOWSHIP.

Yea, by my fay! To God I betake thee.

EVERYMAN.

Farewell, good Fellowship! for thee my heart is sore.
Adieu for ever! I shall see thee no more.   300

FELLOWSHIP.

In faith, Everyman, farewell now at the ending.
For you I will remember that parting is mourning.

[*Exit* FELLOWSHIP.]

EVERYMAN.
 Alack! shall we thus depart indeed –
 Ah, Lady, help! – without any more comfort?
 Lo, Fellowship forsaketh me in my most need. 305
 For help in this world whither shall I resort?
 Fellowship herebefore with me would merry make,
 And now little sorrow for me doth he take.
 It is said, 'In prosperity men friends may find,
 Which in adversity be full unkind.' 310
 Now whither for succour shall I flee,
 Sith that Fellowship hath forsaken me?
 To my kinsmen I will, truly,
 Praying them to help me in my necessity.
 I believe that they will do so, 315
 For 'Kind will creep where it may not go.'
 I will go say, for yonder I see them.
 Where be ye now, my friends and kinsmen?

[*Enter* KINDRED *and* COUSIN.]

KINDRED.
 Here be we now at your commandment.
 Cousin, I pray you show us your intent 320
 In any wise, and not spare.

COUSIN.
 Yea, Everyman, and to us declare
 If ye be disposed to go anywhither.
 For, wit you well, we will live and die together.

KINDRED.

    In wealth and woe we will with you hold,   325
    For over his kin a man may be bold.

EVERYMAN.

    Gramercy, my friends and kinsmen kind!
    Now shall I show you the grief of my mind.
    I was commanded by a messenger,
    That is a high king's chief officer;   330
    He bade me go a pilgrimage, to my pain,
    And I know well I shall never come again.
    Also I must give a reckoning strait,
    For I have a great enemy that hath me in wait,
    Which intendeth me for to hinder.   335

KINDRED.

    What account is that which ye must render?
    That would I know.

EVERYMAN.

    Of all my works I must show
    How I have lived and my days spent;
    Also of ill deeds that I have used   340
    In my time, sith life was me lent,
    And of all virtues that I have refused.
    Therefore, I pray you, go thither with me
    To help to make mine account, for saint charity.

COUSIN.

    What, to go thither? Is that the matter?   345
    Nay, Everyman, I had liefer fast bread and water
    All this five year and more!

EVERYMAN.

    Alas, that ever I was bore!

    For now shall I never be merry,

    If that you forsake me.   350

KINDRED.

    Ah, sir, what? Ye be a merry man!

    Take good heart to you, and make no moan.

    But one thing I warn you, by Saint Anne:

    As for me, ye shall go alone.

EVERYMAN.

    My Cousin, will you not with me go?   355

COUSIN.

    No, by our Lady! I have the cramp in my toe.

    Trust not to me, for, so God me speed,

    I will deceive you in your most need.

KINDRED.

    It availeth not us to tice.

    Ye shall have my maid with all my heart;   360

    She loveth to go to feasts, there to be nice,

    And to dance, and abroad to start.

    I will give her leave to help you in that journey,

    If that you and she may agree.

EVERYMAN.

    Now show me the very effect of your mind;   365

    Will you go with me or abide behind?

KINDRED.

    Abide behind? Yea, that will I, and I may.
    Therefore farewell till another day!

[*Exit* KINDRED.]

EVERYMAN.

    How should I be merry or glad?
    For fair promises men to me make,   370
    But when I have most need they me forsake.
    I am deceived; that maketh me sad.

COUSIN.

    Cousin Everyman, farewell now!
    For, verily, I will not go with you.
    Also of mine own an unready reckoning   375
    I have to account; therefore I make tarrying.
    Now God keep thee, for now I go.

[*Exit* COUSIN.]

EVERYMAN.

    Ah, Jesus, is all come hereto?
    Lo, fair words maketh fools fain.
    They promise and nothing will do, certain.   380
    My kinsmen promised me faithfully
    For to abide with me steadfastly,
    And now fast away do they flee;
    Even so Fellowship promised me.
    What friend were best me of to provide?   385
    I lose my time here longer to abide.
    Yet in my mind a thing there is!

All my life I have loved riches;
If that my Good now help me might,
He would make my heart full light.   390
I will speak to him in this distress –
Where art thou, my Goods and richesse?

GOODS.

Who calleth me? Everyman? What! hast thou haste?
I lie here in corners, trussed and piled so high,
And in chests I am locked so fast,   395
Also sacked in bags – thou mayst see with thine eye
I cannot stir – in packs low I lie.
What would ye have? Lightly me say.

EVERYMAN.

Come hither, Good, in all the haste thou may,
For of counsel I must desire thee.   400

[GOODS *goes forward.*]

GOODS.

Sir, and ye in the world have sorrow or adversity,
That can I help you to remedy shortly.

EVERYMAN.

It is another disease that grieveth me;
In this world it is not, I tell thee so.
I am sent for, another way to go,   405
To give a strait count general
Before the highest Jupiter of all.
And all my life I have had joy and pleasure in thee;
Therefore, I pray thee, go with me;

For, peradventure, thou mayst before God almighty   410
My reckoning help to clean and purify;
For it is said ever among
That 'Money maketh all right that is wrong.'

GOODS.

Nay, Everyman, I sing another song.
I follow no man in such voyages;   415
For, and I went with thee,
Thou shouldest fare much the worse for me;
For, because on me thou did set thy mind,
Thy reckoning I have made blotted and blind,
That thine account thou cannot make truly;   420
And that hast thou for the love of me.

EVERYMAN.

That would grieve me full sore,
When I should come to that fearful answer.
Up, let us go thither together!

GOODS.

Nay, not so! I am too brittle; I may not endure.   425
I will follow no man one foot, be ye sure.

EVERYMAN.

Alas, I have thee loved, and had great pleasure
All my life-days on good and treasure.

GOODS.

That is to thy damnation, without leasing,
For my love is contrary to the love everlasting.   430
But, if thou had me loved moderately during,

As to the poor give part of me,
Then shouldest thou not in this dolour be,
Nor in this great sorrow and care.

EVERYMAN.
Lo, now was I deceived ere I was ware,   435
And all I may wite my spending of time.

GOODS.
What, weenest thou that I am thine?

EVERYMAN.
I had wend so.

GOODS.
Nay, Everyman, I say no.
As for a while I was lent thee;   440
A season thou hast had me in prosperity.
My condition is man's soul to kill;
If I save one, a thousand I do spill.
Weenest thou that I will follow thee?
Nay, fro this world not, verily.   445

EVERYMAN.
I had wend otherwise.

GOODS.
Therefore to thy soul Good is a thief,
For when thou art dead, this is my guise:
Another to deceive in this same wise
As I have done thee, and all to his soul's reprefe.   450

EVERYMAN.
O false Good, cursed thou be,
Thou traitor to God, that hast deceived me
And caught me in thy snare!

GOODS.
Marry, thou brought thyself in care,
Whereof I am glad.   455
I must needs laugh; I cannot be sad.

EVERYMAN.
Ah, Good, thou hast had long my heartly love!
I gave thee that which should be the Lord's above.
But wilt thou not go with me indeed?
I pray thee truth to say.   460

GOODS.
No, so God me speed!
Therefore farewell, and have good day!

[*Exit* GOODS.]

EVERYMAN.
O, to whom shall I make my moan
For to go with me in that heavy journey?
First Fellowship said he would with me gone;   465
His words were very pleasant and gay,
But afterward he left me alone.
Then spake I to my kinsmen, all in despair,
And also they gave me words fair;
They lacked no fair speaking,   470
But all forsake me in the ending.

Then went I to my Goods, that I loved best,
In hope to have comfort, but there had I least;
For my Goods sharply did me tell
That he bringeth many into hell. 475
Then of myself I was ashamed;
And so I am worthy to be blamed.
Thus may I well myself hate.
Of whom shall I now counsel take?
I think that I shall never speed 480
Till that I go to my Good Deed.
But, alas, she is so weak
That she can neither go nor speak.
Yet will I venture on her now.
My Good Deeds, where be you? 485

GOOD DEEDS.

Here I lie; cold in the ground
Thy sins hath me sore bound,
That I cannot stir.

EVERYMAN.

O Good Deeds, I stand in fear.
I must you pray of counsel, 490
For help now should come right well.

GOOD DEEDS.

Everyman, I have understanding
That ye be summoned account to make
Before Messias, of Jerusalem King.
And you do by me, that journey with you will I take. 495

EVERYMAN.
    Therefore I come to you, my moan to make;
    I pray you that ye will go with me.

GOOD DEEDS.
    I would full fain, but I cannot stand, verily.

EVERYMAN.
    Why, is there anything on you fall?

GOOD DEEDS.
    Yea, sir, I may thank you of all.   500
    If ye had perfectly cheered me,
    Your book of count full ready had be.

    [*Shows* EVERYMAN *his books of account.*]

    Look, the books of your works and deeds eke,
    As how they lie under the feet,
    To your soul's heaviness!   505

EVERYMAN.
    Our Lord Jesus help me,
    For one letter here I cannot see!

GOOD DEEDS.
    Here is a blind reckoning in time of distress!

EVERYMAN.
    Good Deeds, I pray you help me in this need,
    Or else I am for ever damned, indeed;   510
    Therefore help me to make reckoning

Before the Redeemer of all thing,
That King is, and was, and ever shall.

GOOD DEEDS.

Everyman, I am sorry of your fall,
And fain would I help you, and I were able.   515

EVERYMAN.

Good Deeds, your counsel I pray you give me.

GOOD DEEDS.

That shall I do verily:
Though that on my feet I may not go,
I have a sister that shall with you also,
Called Knowledge, which shall with you abide,   520
To help you to make that dreadful reckoning.

[*Enter* KNOWLEDGE.]

KNOWLEDGE.

Everyman, I will go with thee, and be thy guide,
In thy most need to go by thy side.

EVERYMAN.

In good condition I am now in every thing,
And am wholly content with this good thing,   525
Thanked be God my creator!

GOOD DEEDS.

And when she hath brought you there
Where thou shalt heal thee of thy smart,

Then go you with your reckoning and your Good
    Deeds together,
For to make you joyful at heart   530
Before the blessed Trinity.

EVERYMAN.
  My Good Deeds, gramercy!
  I am well content, certainly,
  With your words sweet.

KNOWLEDGE.
  Now go we together lovingly   535
  To Confession, that cleansing river.

EVERYMAN.
  For joy I weep! I would we were there!
  But, I pray you, give me cognition
  Where dwelleth that holy man, Confession.

KNOWLEDGE.
  In the House of Salvation –   540
  We shall find him in that place,
  That shall us comfort, by God's grace.

[CONFESSION *is seen at a distance within
the House of Salvation.* KNOWLEDGE *leads*
EVERYMAN *there.*]

Lo, this is Confession. Kneel down and ask mercy,
For he is in good conceit with God Almighty.

EVERYMAN.

O glorious fountain, that all uncleanness doth clarify, 545
Wash fro me the spots of vice unclean,
That on me no sin may be seen.
I come with Knowledge for my redemption,
Redempt with heart and full contrition,
For I am commanded a pilgrimage to take, 550
And great accounts before God to make.
Now I pray you, Shrift, mother of salvation,
Help my Good Deeds, for my piteous exclamation!

CONFESSION.

I know your sorrow well, Everyman.
Because with Knowledge ye come to me, 555
I will you comfort as well as I can,
And a precious jewel I will give thee,
Called penance, voider of adversity.
Therewith shall your body chastised be,
With abstinence and perseverance in God's service. 560

[*Shows* EVERYMAN *the scourge of penance.*]

Here shall you receive that scourge of me,
Which is penance strong that ye must endure,
To remember thy Saviour was scourged for thee
With sharp scourges, and suffered it patiently;
So must thou, ere thou scape that painful pilgrimage. 565
Knowledge, keep him in this voyage,
And by that time Good Deeds will be with thee.
But in any wise be sicker of mercy,
For your time draweth fast. And ye will saved be,
Ask God mercy, and he will grant truly. 570

When with the scourge of penance man doth him bind,
The oil of forgiveness then shall he find.

EVERYMAN.
Thanked be God for his gracious work,
For now I will my penance begin.
This hath rejoiced and lighted my heart,   575
Though the knots be painful and hard within.

KNOWLEDGE.
Everyman, look your penance that ye fulfil,
What pain that ever it to you be,
And Knowledge shall give you counsel at will
How your account ye shall make clearly.   580

EVERYMAN.
O eternal God, O heavenly figure,
O way of righteousness, O goodly vision –
Which descended down in a virgin pure
Because he would every man redeem,
Which Adam forfeited by his disobedience –   585
O blessed godhead, elect and high divine,
Forgive my grievous offence!
Here I cry thee mercy in this presence.
O ghostly treasure, O ransomer and redeemer,
Of all the world hope and conduiter,   590
Mirror of joy, foundator of mercy,
Which enlumineth heaven and earth thereby,
Hear my clamorous complaint, though it late be;
Receive my prayers, unworthy in this heavy life.
Though I be a sinner most abominable,   595
Yet let my name be written in Moses' table!

O Mary, pray to the maker of all thing,
Me for to help at my ending,
And save me fro the power of my enemy,
For Death assaileth me strongly;   600
And, Lady, that I may, by mean of thy prayer,
Of your son's glory to be partner,
By the means of his passion, I it crave.
I beseech you help my soul to save.
Knowledge, give me the scourge of penance;   605
My flesh therewith shall have acquaintance.

[*He strips off his fine clothes and takes the scourge.*]

I will now begin, if God give me grace.

KNOWLEDGE.
    Everyman, God give you time and space!
    Thus I bequeath you in the hands of our Saviour.
    Now may you make your reckoning sure.   610

EVERYMAN.
    In the name of the Holy Trinity,
    My body sore punished shall be.
    Take this, body, for the sin of the flesh!

[*He scourges himself.*]

Also, thou delightest to go gay and fresh,
And in the way of damnation thou did me bring;   615
Therefore suffer now strokes of punishing.
Now of penance I will wade the water clear,
To save me from purgatory, that sharp fire.

[GOOD DEEDS *arises.*]

GOOD DEEDS.
    I thank God! now I can walk and go,
    And am delivered of my sickness and woe;   620
    Therefore with Everyman I will go, and not spare.
    His good works I will help him to declare.

KNOWLEDGE.
    Now, Everyman, be merry and glad!
    Your Good Deeds cometh; now ye may not be sad.
    Now is your Good Deeds whole and sound,   625
    Going upright upon the ground.

EVERYMAN.
    My heart is light, and shall be evermore!
    Now will I smite faster than I did before.

[*He scourges himself again.*]

GOOD DEEDS.
    Everyman, pilgrim, my special friend,
    Blessed be thou without end.   630
    For thee is preparate the eternal glory.
    Ye have me made whole and sound;
    Therefore I will bide by thee in every stound.

EVERYMAN.
    Welcome, my Good Deeds! Now I hear thy voice,
    I weep for very sweetness of love.   635

KNOWLEDGE.

Be no more sad, but ever rejoice!
God seeth thy living in his throne above.

[KNOWLEDGE *gives* EVERYMAN *the garment
of contrition.*]

Put on this garment to thy behove,
Which is wet with your tears,
Or else before God you may it miss,   640
When ye to your journey's end come shall.

EVERYMAN.

Gentle Knowledge, what do ye it call?

KNOWLEDGE.

It is a garment of sorrow;
Fro pain it will you borrow;
Contrition it is,   645
That geteth forgiveness.
It pleaseth God passing well.

GOOD DEEDS.

Everyman, will you wear it for your heal?

[EVERYMAN *puts on the garment.*]

EVERYMAN.

Now blessed be Jesu, Mary's son,
For now have I on true contrition;   650
And let us go now without tarrying.
Good Deeds, have we clear our reckoning?

GOOD DEEDS.
  Yea, indeed, I have it here.

EVERYMAN.
  Then I trust we need not fear.
  Now, friends, let us not part in twain.   655

KNOWLEDGE.
  Nay, Everyman, that will we not, certain.

GOOD DEEDS.
  Yet must thou lead with thee
  Three persons of great might.

EVERYMAN.
  Who should they be?

GOOD DEEDS.
  Discretion and Strength they hight,   660
  And thy Beauty may not abide behind.

KNOWLEDGE.
  Also ye must call to mind
  Your Five Wits as for your counsellors.

GOOD DEEDS.
  You must have them ready at all hours.

EVERYMAN.
  How shall I get them hither?   665

KNOWLEDGE.
    You must call them all together,
    And they will hear you incontinent.

EVERYMAN.
    My friends, come hither and be present,
    Discretion, Strength, my Five Wits, and Beauty.

    [*Enter* DISCRETION, STRENGTH, FIVE WITS,
    and BEAUTY.]

BEAUTY.
    Here at your will we be all ready;   670
    What will ye that we should do?

GOOD DEEDS.
    That ye would with Everyman go,
    And help him in his pilgrimage.
    Advise you, will ye with him or not in that voyage?

STRENGTH.
    We will bring him all thither,   675
    To his help and comfort, ye may believe me.

DISCRETION.
    So will we go with him all together.

EVERYMAN.
    Almighty God, lofed may thou be!
    I give thee laud that I have hither brought
    Strength, Discretion, Beauty, and Five Wits – lack
        I nought –   680

And my Good Deeds, with Knowledge clear;
All be in my company at my will here.
I desire no more to my business.

STRENGTH.
And I, Strength, will by you stand in distress,
Though thou would in battle fight on the ground.   685

FIVE WITS.
And though it were through the world round,
We will not depart, for sweet ne sour.

BEAUTY.
No more will I, unto death's hour,
Whatsoever thereof befall.

DISCRETION.
Everyman, advise you first of all;   690
Go with a good advisement and deliberation.
We all give you virtuous monition
That all shall be well.

EVERYMAN.
My friends, harken what I will tell —
I pray God reward you in his heavenly sphere —   695
Now harken, all that be here,
For I will make my testament
Here before you all present.
In alms half my good I will give with my hands twain
In the way of charity, with good intent,   700

And the other half still shall remain
In queth, to be returned there it ought to be.
This I do in despite of the fiend of hell,
To go quit out of his peril
Ever after and this day.   705

KNOWLEDGE.

Everyman, harken what I say!
Go to Priesthood, I you advise,
And receive of him in any wise
The holy sacrament and ointment together;
Then shortly see ye turn again hither.   710
We will all abide you here.

FIVE WITS.

Yea, Everyman, hie you that ye ready were.
There is no emperor, king, duke, ne baron,
That of God hath commission
As hath at least priest in the world being.   715
For of the blessed sacraments pure and benign
He beareth the keys, and thereof hath the cure
For man's redemption − it is ever sure −
Which God, for our soul's medicine
Gave us out of his heart with great pain.   720
Here in this transitory life, for thee and me
The blessed sacraments seven there be −
Baptism, confirmation, with priesthood good,
And the sacrament of God's precious flesh and blood,
Marriage, the holy extreme unction, and penance −   725
These seven be good to have in remembrance
Gracious sacraments of high divinity.

EVERYMAN.
  Fain would I receive that holy body,
  And meekly to my ghostly father I will go.

FIVE WITS.
  Everyman, that is the best that ye can do.   730
  God will you to salvation bring,
  For priesthood exceedeth all other thing.
  To us holy scripture they do teach,
  And converteth man from sin heaven to reach.
  God hath to them more power given   735
  Than to any angel that is in heaven.
  With five words he may consecrate,
  God's body in flesh and blood to make,
  And handleth his maker between his hands.
  The priest bindeth and unbindeth all bands,   740
  Both in earth and in heaven.
  Thou ministers of all the sacraments seven
  Though we kiss thy feet, thou were worthy.
  Thou art surgeon that cureth sin deadly.
  No remedy we find under God   745
  But all only priesthood.
  Everyman, God gave priests that dignity,
  And setteth them in his stead among us to be;
  Thus be they above angels in degree.

[*Exit* EVERYMAN, *to receive the sacrament and extreme
unction from the priest.*]

KNOWLEDGE.
  If priests be good, it is so, surely.   750
  But when Jesu hanged on the cross with great smart,

There he gave out of his blessed heart
The same sacrament, in great torment.
He sold them not to us, that Lord omnipotent.
Therefore Saint Peter the apostle doth say   755
That Jesu's curse hath all they
Which God their Saviour do buy or sell,
Or they for any money do take or tell.
Sinful priests giveth the sinners example bad;
Their children sitteth by other men's fires, I have heard,
And some haunteth women's company   761
With unclean life, as lusts of lechery.
These be with sin made blind.

FIVE WITS.
I trust to God no such may we find;
Therefore let us priesthood honour,   765
And follow their doctrine for our souls' succour.
We be their sheep, and they shepherds be,
By whom we all be kept in surety.
Peace! for yonder I see Everyman come,
Which hath made true satisfaction.   770

GOOD DEEDS.
Methink it is he, indeed.

[*Enter* EVERYMAN, *with a crucifix.*]

EVERYMAN.
Now Jesu be your alder speed!
I have received the sacrament for my redemption,
And then mine extreme unction.
Blessed be all they that counselled me to take it!   775

And now, friends, let us go without longer respite.
I thank God that ye have tarried so long.
Now set each of you on this rood your hand,
And shortly follow me.
I go before there I would be. God be our guide!   780

[*They grasp the crucifix in turn.*]

STRENGTH.

Everyman, we will not fro you go
Till ye have done this voyage long.

DISCRETION.

I, Discretion, will bide by you also.

KNOWLEDGE.

And though this pilgrimage be never so strong,
I will never part you fro.   785

STRENGTH.

Everyman, I will be as sure by thee
As ever I did by Judas Maccabee.

[*They journey to* EVERYMAN'*s grave.*]

EVERYMAN.

Alas, I am so faint I may not stand!
My limbs under me doth fold.
Friends, let us not turn again to this land,   790
Not for all the world's gold,
For into this cave must I creep
And turn to earth, and there to sleep.

BEAUTY.
What, into this grave? Alas!

EVERYMAN.
Yea, there shall ye consume, more and less.   795

BEAUTY.
And what, should I smother here?

EVERYMAN.
Yea, by my faith, and never more appear.
In this world live no more we shall,
But in heaven before the highest Lord of all.

BEAUTY.
I cross out all this! Adieu, by Saint John!   800
I take my tap in my lap, and am gone.

EVERYMAN.
What, Beauty, whither will ye ?

BEAUTY.
Peace! I am deaf; I look not behind me,
Not and thou wouldest give me all the gold in thy chest.

[*Exit* BEAUTY.]

EVERYMAN.
Alas, whereto may I trust?   805
Beauty goeth fast away fro me.
She promised with me to live and die.

STRENGTH.

    Everyman, I will thee also forsake and deny.

    Thy game liketh me not at all.

EVERYMAN.

    Why, then, ye will forsake me all?   810

    Sweet Strength, tarry a little space!

STRENGTH.

    Nay, sir, by the rood of grace!

    I will hie me from thee fast,

    Though thou weep till thy heart to-brast.

EVERYMAN.

    Ye would ever bide by me, ye said.   815

STRENGTH.

    Yea, I have you far enough conveyed.

    Ye be old enough, I understand,

    Your pilgrimage to take on hand.

    I repent me that I hither came.

EVERYMAN.

    Strength, you to displease I am to blame;   820

    Yet promise is debt – this ye well wot.

STRENGTH.

    In faith, I care not.

    Thou art but a fool to complain.

    You spend your speech and waste your brain.

    Go thrust thee into the ground!

[*Exit* STRENGTH.]   825

EVERYMAN.
   I had wend surer I should you have found.
   He that trusteth in his Strength
   She him deceiveth at the length.
   Both Strength and Beauty forsaketh me,
   Yet they promised me fair and lovingly.   830

DISCRETION.
   Everyman, I will after Strength be gone;
   As for me, I will leave you alone.

EVERYMAN.
   Why, Discretion, will ye forsake me?

DISCRETION.
   Yea, in faith, I will go fro thee,
   For when Strength goeth before   835
   I follow after evermore.

EVERYMAN.
   Yet, I pray thee, for the love of the Trinity,
   Look in my grave once piteously.

DISCRETION.
   Nay, so nigh will I not come!
   Farewell, everychone!

[*Exit* DISCRETION.]   840

EVERYMAN.
    O, all thing faileth, save God alone –
    Beauty, Strength, and Discretion –
    For when Death bloweth his blast
    They all run fro me full fast.

FIVE WITS.
    Everyman, my leave now of thee I take;   845
    I will follow the other, for here I thee forsake.

EVERYMAN.
    Alas, then may I wail and weep,
    For I took you for my best friend.

FIVE WITS.
    I will no longer thee keep.
    Now farewell, and there an end.

    [*Exit* FIVE WITS.]   850

EVERYMAN.
    O Jesu, help! All hath forsaken me.

GOOD DEEDS.
    Nay, Everyman, I will bide with thee.
    I will not forsake thee indeed.
    Thou shalt find me a good friend at need.

EVERYMAN.
    Gramercy, Good Deeds! Now may I true friends see. 855
    They have forsaken me, everychone.

I loved them better than my Good Deeds alone.
Knowledge, will ye forsake me also?

KNOWLEDGE.

Yea, Everyman, when ye to death shall go;
But not yet, for no manner of danger. 860

EVERYMAN.

Gramercy, Knowledge, with all my heart.

KNOWLEDGE.

Nay, yet I will not from hence depart
Till I see where ye shall be come.

EVERYMAN.

Methink, alas, that I must be gone,
To make my reckoning and my debts pay, 865
For I see my time is nigh spent away.
Take example, all ye that this do hear or see,
How they that I loved best do forsake me,
Except my Good Deeds that bideth truly.

GOOD DEEDS.

All earthly things is but vanity – 870
Beauty, Strength, and Discretion do man forsake,
Foolish friends, and kinsmen, that fair spake –
All fleeth save Good Deeds, and that am I.

EVERYMAN.

Have mercy on me, God most mighty,
And stand by me, thou mother and maid, holy Mary! 875

GOOD DEEDS.
   Fear not. I will speak for thee.

EVERYMAN.
   Here I cry God mercy!

GOOD DEEDS.
   Short our end, and minish our pain.
   Let us go and never come again.

EVERYMAN.
   Into thy hands, Lord, my soul I commend!   880
   Receive it, Lord, that it be not lost!
   As thou me boughtest, so me defend,
   And save me from the fiend's boast,
   That I may appear with that blessed host
   That shall be saved at the day of doom.   885
   In manus tuas, of mights most
   For ever, *commendo spiritum meum*.

   [EVERYMAN *and* GOOD DEEDS *disappear into
   the grave.*]

KNOWLEDGE.
   Now hath he suffered that we all shall endure.
   The Good Deeds shall make all sure.

   [*Angelic music. An* ANGEL *appears in a high place with*
   EVERYMAN'*s Book of Reckoning, and receives the soul,
   which has risen from the grave.*]

Now hath he made ending. 890
Methinketh that I hear angels sing
And make great joy and melody
Where Everyman's soul received shall be.

ANGEL.

Come, excellent elect spouse, to Jesu!
Hereabove thou shalt go 895
Because of thy singular virtue.
Now the soul is taken the body fro,
Thy reckoning is crystal clear.
Now shalt thou into the heavenly sphere,
Unto the which all ye shall come 900
That liveth well before the day of doom.

[ANGEL *withdraws. Enter* DOCTOR, *as epilogue.*]

DOCTOR.

This moral men may have in mind.
Ye hearers, take it of worth, old and young.
And forsake Pride, for he deceiveth you in the end. 904
And remember Beauty, Five Wits, Strength, and
   Discretion –
They all at the last do every man forsake,
Save his Good Deeds there doth he take.
But beware! And they be small,
Before God he hath no help at all;
None excuse may be there for every man. 910
Alas, how shall he do then?
For after death amends may no man make,
For then Mercy and Pity doth him forsake.

If his reckoning be not clear when he doth come,
God will say, '*Ite, maledicti, in ignem aeternum.*'   915
And he that hath his account whole and sound,
High in heaven he shall be crowned –
Unto which place God bring us all thither,
That we may live body and soul together.
Thereto help the Trinity!   920
Amen, say ye, for saint charity!

[*Exit.*]

Finis.

*Thus endeth this moral play of Everyman, imprinted in Paul's
Churchyard by me John Skot.*

Glossary

Adonai – (Hebrew) Lord
advisement – deliberation
affiance – trust
alder speed, your – the support of you all
and – (at line 292, etc) if
appaireth – decays, declines
availeth . . . tice – no use enticing us
behove – benefit
beset – set about
blind – strange, unknown
bore – born
bring me forward – go forward with me
caitiff – base fellow
commendo spiritum meum – (Latin) 'I commend my spirit'
conceit – esteem
conduiter – conductor
count – account
covetise – covetousness, greed
dolour – sadness
dreadeth, that no man – that fears no one
eke – also
everychone – everyone
fain – joyous
fall, on you – happened to you

fay – faith
fear – (at line 253) frighten
for – (at line 170) lest, in case
forbear – allow, tolerate
foundator – founder, originator
get, be – been born
gramercy – thank you
hight – are named
In manus tuas – (Latin) 'into thy hands'
incontinent – immediately
Ite . . . aeternum – (Latin) 'Depart, you cursed, into everlasting fire'
Judas Maccabee – Judas Maccabeus, a leader of the Jews
Kind . . . grow – kinship will be faithful in face of adversity
laud – praise
leasing – lying
liefer – rather
lofed – praised
Messias – Messiah
minish – alleviate, diminish
monition – warning
Moses' table – the tablet of penance, one of the two brought down by Moses from Mount Sinai
nature, of – in the course of nature, in due course
ne . . . ne – neither . . . nor
needs – necessarily
nice – bawdy, wanton
outsearch – seek out
pardie – by God
peradventure – perhaps
preparate – prepared
queth, remain in – be kept aside to make restitution

reprefe – disgrace
rest – arrest, detain
richesse – riches, wealth
rood of grace – Christ's cross
short our end – shorten our dying
sicker – sure, certain
sith – since, because
stound, in every – always
strait – exact, precise
tap in my lap, take my – proverbial, gather up my baggage and
    be gone
tide – time
to-brast – break into pieces
voider – remover
ware – aware
weenest – think
wend – (verb) thought
wit – (verb) know, (noun) knowledge, mind
wise – (at line 449) manner, way
wite – blame on
wot – know